Elsewhere

20/2/20

To Sandy,

I hope you enjoy this virtual globe trot!

Maeve O'S.

Other books by Maeve O'Sullivan
from Alba Publishing:

Double Rainbow* (haiku), with Kim Richardson (2005)

Initial Response, an A-Z of Haiku Moments* (2011)

*Vocal Chord*s – poetry (2014)

A Train Hurtles West - haiku (2015)

* Both of these titles are out of print but available to download from The Haiku Foundation's Digital Library (www.thehaikufoundation.org)

Elsewhere

around the world in poetry, haiku & haibun

Maeve O'Sullivan

Alba Publishing

Published by Alba Publishing,
P O Box 266, Uxbridge
UB9 5NX, United Kingdom
www.albapublishing.com

© 2017 Maeve O'Sullivan
All rights reserved
No part of this publication may be reproduced, stored in a retrieval system, or transmitted by any form or by any means electronic, mechanical, photocopying, recording or otherwise without the prior written permission of the copyright owners.

A catalogue record for this book is available from the British Library

ISBN: 978-1-910185-77-3

Edited, designed and typeset by Kim Richardson
Cover image of Kompukuji temple, Kyoto, Japan © Maeve O'Sullivan,
Printed by Essentra, Dublin, Ireland

10 9 8 7 6 5 4 3

Donation:
30% of the profits from sales of this book will go to Friends of the Earth Ireland, a non-profit organisation which campaigns for environmental justice and sustainability and is part of the world's largest network of environmental groups. www.foe.ie

In memory of my sister Jean O'Sullivan (1954-2017), who was similarly affected by the travel bug and similarly lacking the shyness gene. *¡Buen camino, hermana!*

*We shall not cease from exploration
And the end of all our exploring
Will be to arrive where we started
And know the place for the first time.*

T.S. Eliot, from *Four Quartets*

Contents

Author's Preface	10
I Home	13
Apples and Oranges	14
Manicure	15
Dun Laoghaire	17
Fourteen Days	18
Closure	19
Funeral Season	21
Dublin	23
Night Walking, November 2015	27
Outside the Pale	28
Spirit of Killaloe	30
II West	31
Leaving Vigo	32
Europe	33
Inside Room 102	35
Gijón, Asturias	36
Mother-to-be	38
Peregrina	39
Slow Camino	40
Santiago de Compostela	45
Southern California	47
Silverlake	49
Peru	50
A Morning in Yacango	53

Ecuador	54
Galápagos Islands	57
Dateline Quito	59
Scenes from Peru and Ecuador	60
Colombia	62
The Rules of Salsa	65
Santiago, Chile	66
III East	**67**
Resettled	68
Japan	70
A Slice of Autumn	73
Hong Kong	75
Kathmandu	77
Buddhas of Asia	78
New Delhi	79
New Year at Rumtek Monastery	80
Sikkim Retreat	81
Morning Practice	85
Agra	86
Varanasi	88
Mumbai	90
Endangered	91
Sri Lanka	92
Barcelona	94
Magnus's Digit	95
Can Serrat / Montserrat	96
Thinking about our Bodies at the Rodin Museum	98
A Lapsed Catholic's Prayer	99

Envoi – Back Home	101
Settling	102
Wild Atlantic Way	104
Glossary	**106**
Acknowledgements & Thanks	**107**
About the Author	**110**

Author's Preface

This book marks the completion of a life-changing world trip, about which I had been dreaming for many years. A confluence of circumstances made this grand tour possible, some of which will be apparent from Home, the first section of the book. Most of the work in Home was written in the period between the publication of my most recent collections, *Vocal Chords* (2014) and *A Train Hurtles West* (2015), and the start of this particular series of journeys. The next two sections of the work – bar a few poems and haiku, divided into West and East and comprising the majority of the book – were inspired by the travels which took place from the start of September 2016 to the end of May 2017. The loss of both parents in recent years, and the subsequent sale of the family home, preceded this trip. Sadly we also lost our sister Jean to cancer just three months after my return home, hence the book's dedication. Along with Maurice, Mairéad, and my dear friend Bruce, Jean is now elsewhere.

During my travels, I visited thirteen countries across four continents, only two of which I had spent any time in before (France and Spain). An *envoi* presents haiku produced in the summer after my return to Ireland. Although I visited friends and family along the way – as well as friends of family and family of friends – and participated in a number of group tours, this was essentially a solo trip. Other outcomes of it include lots of new memories, friends and photos from 'elsewhere', one of which graces the cover.

In this, my fourth collection, I've done something that I haven't done before: presented haiku and long-form poems together, with the addition of some haibun, a form which combines prose and haiku. I've done this because the work is unified in its overall theme of home-travel-home, so it didn't make sense to separate them out into different books. I also believe that *haikai* – haiku and related forms – shouldn't be confined to a quasi-ghetto in the wider poetry world, with (predominantly) separate journals, competitions, representative organisations, and activities. I hope this book will help to further integrate it a little, along with publications by other *haijin*-poets which have gone before, and those which will hopefully follow.

Maeve O'Sullivan,
53.35° N, 6.26° W
September 2017

I Home

Apples and Oranges

It's a warm June afternoon. I'm waiting for a suburban train to take me to Glenageary station. I am eleven. On the platform near me is a Loreto nun in her black habit, a resident of the convent attached to my primary school whose playground has a view of Dalkey Island. I start to peel an orange from my lunchbox. She recognises me and asks me which secondary school I'll be attending in the autumn.

My parents have decided to send me to a new non fee-paying comprehensive rather than the Loreto secondary school in Dalkey, which two of my older sisters attended. I tell her this. The new school is located in a less salubrious suburb of South County Dublin, and managed by a progressive lay headmistress.

The nun's response is this: *You'd be the kind of girl to go to a comprehensive alright. What do you mean, Sister?*, I ask, puzzled. *Eating an orange in public,* she replies.

        first assembly   a sea of green gaberdine

Manicure

This is a springtime poem for you, mother,
about the happenings of last Christmas
when you had to leave the family home
after a fall. In hospital for a cure,
you left behind the unopened gifts,
your husband, the house and your life.

Music's been a big part of your life.
The Lehmann, a bequest from your mother,
kick-started many sing-songs, a true gift;
taking turns, with harmonies at Christmas.
Now the doctors are administering their cure,
and we're hoping you'll soon be home.

It's strange not having you at home,
where the accoutrements of your life
lie all around. We're in need of a cure
to ease your absence, mother.
You were missing at Christmas
your blank new diary, our gifts.

I've kept all your letters and gifts
in the various places I've called home,
and every year a sweet card at Christmas.
You've nurtured me throughout my life,
now it's my turn to try and mother
you, my role to heal and cure.

Less of the manic and more of the cure
was what you said when I gave you gifts
of nail clippers and emery board, mother,
that day when your mind was clearly home.
No guarantee it will stay that way for life,
let alone until next Christmas.

Where will you be next Christmas?
Will you still be seeking to cure
The late depredations of this life
that you've lived, so rich in gifts?
Will you be back in your own home,
or in another suitable for grandmother?

Mother, your best gifts didn't come
Christmas-wrapped: your lifestyle,
your place in your own home secure.

Dun Laoghaire

Killiney Hill –
a southbound Dart
snakes into gorse

rainy afternoon –
only the nettles to tell us
it's summer

Bullock quay wall   its winter benches unencumbered

at the pier's end   an inverted bell   the silent foghorn

Fourteen Days

Mother has stopped eating
I google what happens next:
others who have done this
survive around fourteen days.

I google what happens next:
hunger-strikers and anorexics
survive around fourteen days,
declining to drink water.

Hunger-strikers and anorexics
turn their faces to the wall,
decline drinking water,
refuse all foodstuffs.

She has turned her face to the wall
though she seems quite serene:
refusing all foodstuffs,
just lying in her bed.

She seems quite serene,
like others who have done this,
just lying in her bed –
our mother has stopped eating.

Closure

Over several months, my siblings and I set about clearing the house which was our family home for almost sixty years, from the day my newly-wed parents used their first set of keys, to that other day when my Dad was admitted to hospital, never to return. My mother died four years later, in a nursing home a few miles further south.

> her bony back
> against my palm –
> Mother's Day

We start in January and work our way from the top down, first emptying the attic of its contents. There are dusty books, clothes, blankets, boxes of letters, photographs and lots of *bric-à-brac,* legacies of nine people from three generations. The base of an old gramophone has succumbed to the ravages of woodworm. We fill the first of many skip bags. Gradually, over the spring, we work our way through each former living space, first the upstairs bedrooms and bathroom, then the downstairs rooms, kitchen and garage. So many memories.

> SALE AGREED:
> new buttercups thriving
> in the front lawn

In July, we have a 'house-cooling' party, the six of us inviting friends, family and neighbours to mark the end of many decades of gatherings at what was always a hospitable open house. It is a celebration rather than a mourning, a thanksgiving for many happy years spent in this home. A balmy evening allows us to share the long back garden one last time. We consume pizza and wine, both out of boxes, resting on what remains of the furniture. For a while, we reminisce and laugh, then we pass a guitar around and take turns singing until the early hours.

    old kitchen drawer full of unlit birthday candles

In September the sale is closed. My brother Des and I sign the legal documents and hand over all the remaining sets of keys. We keep the wooden house sign which reads *Carraig Bán,* named after White Rock beach where my parents used to court.

        anniversary weekend
        we drive by the old home –
        shiny new windows

Funeral Season

aunt's funeral Mass –
a monk reaches inside his robes
to silence his phone

December burial –
a gust carries a red hat
into the open grave

limo from the graveyard…
I remove a pine needle
from her daughter's hair

on his birthday
a week after the cremation –
tea with his widower

Christmas tree lights blinking
on the large altar –
friend's father's funeral

fifty-something:
the birthday book of my youth
used for deaths now too

Dublin

first-ever taste
of persimmon –
St. Brigit's Day

after the reading…
a cherry blossom petal
on the heel of his shoe

memorial gardens –
all its roses dreaming
of summer blooms

Viking burial ground
commemorating soldiers
planted elsewhere

running late…
the scent of freshly-cut grass
from Croppy's Acre

from the shrub
to the ice-cream bowl…
lemon verbena

Phoenix Park at night:
a fawn moves towards
the meteor shower

summer evening sun flash photo of copper beeches

somewhere a murmuration is missing you   lone starling

an Irish lullaby
for the infant...
kicking throughout

pink contrails
in a baby blue sky –
All Souls' Day

Sandymount Strand –
birds that haven't flown south
huddling together

night of remembrance   the weeping tree meets us outside

winter solstice   a lone swan at Goldenbridge

Night Walking, November 2015
(for the Paris O'Sullivans)

I Dublin

I run into ghosts
of friends – dead and alive –
as I move south on Liffey Street
towards the river.

On Grafton Street, Christmas
chandeliers are switched off.
I feel safe, unlike my sister
in the 11th arrondissement.

II Upperchurch

Pegasus, The Plough
and our hand-held torches
beam the way, as we walk
from Garnakilka to Glown.

Up hills we are losing
heart, losing confidence,
but the sweepers' voices
whisper us onward.

Outside the Pale

Holy Thursday:
the priest puts an altar girl
through her paces

grey day:
poppies not quite ready
to burst red

waxing June moon
pooling silver-gold
on this northern lake

graced
by a single yellow iris –
retreat garden

hunter's moon   fat pink fuchsias still in flower

lane swimming   at the deep end   an abacus

November hill walk
on the downward stretch –
a lone buttercup

Spirit of Killaloe
(i.m. Bruce Carolan, 1953-2015)

The boat leans gently into Lough Derg's swell;
on board, the teen's clear notes drive out the rain.
The lyric – much beyond her short years – tells
a tale of whiskey, solitude and pain.

I want to share this wonderment with you
but then remember that you've upped and left.
She now sings of a friendship close and true
and suddenly I'm all at sea, bereft.

You had a taste for culture, avant-garde:
cult screenings and film festivals your thing;
for all your pals, you went the extra yard,
with humour sharp and that ironic grin.

When afterwards she covets my old coat,
I gift it to her, then step off the boat.

II West

Leaving Vigo
(i.m. of those who lost their lives in the fatal train derailment outside Santiago de Compostela on the 24th July 2013)

With sad and friendly eyes she answers yes
when I ask if Santiago trains are on.
Seventy-five fatalities, or more:
un accidente horrible – she nods.
A message wishes us a pleasant trip,
the carriage has an eerie muffled mood,
its notice says 130 km per hour,
we read our newspapers and phones, subdued.
I see Camino pilgrims stumbling,
their spirits springing up from bloody rails;
fresh donations from *Gallegos* streaming
through some survivors' arteries and veins.
The train conductor doesn't meet my gaze;
at journey's end we disembark with haste.

Europe

coffee al fresco
the horsefly takes
half a bite

human statue:
his companion applies more paint
this sweltering day

peeling a courgette…
the sound of child's play
in another language

boat tour of the port –
a drone generates
the most excitement

balmy night
a swallow dips close
to my breaststroke

city lake –
a moorhen leads her chicks
towards the evening sun

Inside Room 102

of this Art Deco cinema-hotel,
a youngish Orson holds his second wife,
a most erotic black-and-white embrace:
his right hand firmly grasps her pale left arm,
her head tilts slightly back and to the left,
the lips just barely parted with suspense.
The *Lady from Shanghai* is being shot –
a tale of murder, lust, deception, guns –
and Rita's shorter bleach blonde tresses
are framing her new *femme fatale,* Elsa.
Her neck and shoulders are completely bare,
an eyelash casts a shadow on her cheek.
She leans back for the kiss and holds her breath,
then tumbles into drink, dementia, death.

Gijón, Asturias

orientation stroll…
the first sound
a seagull's cry

beneath the café's din
of TV and chatter –
his song

the peacock shakes
his bridal feathers –
city park cage

hilly headland
its giant sculpture
amplifying the sea

artist's former home   its triple-locked steel door

after a week of sharing   a *pas de deux* in the kitchen

rainy evening –
pouring cider from a height
to drink in one gulp

Mother-to-be
(for Mamo)

The drizzle neatly disappears
the dandelion parachutes
which drift across the thoroughfares
as if to say *tempus fugit.*

León knows how to sit and wait
from Roman times through to the Moors
then finally back to *one true faith,*
exporting it to stay secure.

The pregnant Mary stands behind
an altar lit through coloured glass:
no other woman of her kind
so celebrated by the Mass.

She stayed a maid from crib to tomb –
no floating seed attained her womb.

Peregrina

I've got my stick, I've got my shell,
all set for valley and for ridge.
It feels good to be ready, well
enough to make this pilgrimage.
The native oak too soon gives way
to eucalyptus trees, and pine,
from Morgade to Palas de Rei
with birdsong, though, remaining fine.
At Arzúa the rosary's said
while on the street I drink latte
and later on some wine and bread
I share with new friends quiet, chatty.
Soon Santiago looms in view –
the grail of pilgrims, old and new.

Slow Camino

starting point Sarria   birds cheerlead the way

108 kms to go   the mule and I share an apple

two more new friends –
we cross the wide river
into Portomarín

first taste
of the flesh inside the shell –
waymark symbol

cooler today   the scent of roadside fennel

everlasting hill   the squealing of pigs from a truck

walking day done –
I test the staying power
of sticky-back leaves

Ventas de Narón:
my friend with the Achilles heel
catches up

almost reversing into my footfall   lucky spider

approach to Palas de Rei   a robin lands on the path

I stop for a rest
long enough for a small spider
to make a small web

Monday morning –
a grey heron sails over
the furrowed field

I miss the tunnel
under the main road –
bee in a foxglove

mine's a slow Camino...
yours is even slower
stripy caterpillar

eucalyptus trees
in various stages of stripping –
their scent!

ten miles to go   birdsong eclipsed by jet engines

this hill, this heat   *¡Buen Camino, amiga!*

last day of the hike:
the cockerel makes sure
I'm rising and shining

the granite touch
of the cathedral wall –
Danny Boy on fiddle

Santiago de Compostela

Plaza Quintana
glass rosary beads glinting
in the afternoon sun

statue of St. James
a pilgrim's arms appear
to give him a hug

Workers' Square
his steel drum reverberates
to the opposite corner

Ascension Day –
the rich notes of this organ
crawling with cherubs

an elderly priest
enters the confessional –
half door half open

the *botafumiero*
diffuses its incense in wide arcs –
moving

Southern California

Palm Sunday:
a hummingbird drinks his fill
of sugared water

Santa Monica
he skates past the sign:
TSUNAMI HAZARD ZONE

a row of palm silhouettes above Sunset Boulevard

scent of a lemon   just released from its tree

San Diego Bay –
its deep blue darkened
by an aircraft carrier

we three walk
by the empty reservoir –
orange blossom fragrance

a mockingbird
tries out another voice –
Easter Sunday

Silverlake
(after Charles Bukowski)

The cigarette papers have run out
and the store will be closed by now
so I'm doodling on an old wooden board.

There's beer in the fridge, and nuts in a bowl;
oranges and lemons are ripening
out in the back yard.

The hot faucet makes a hullabaloo
and we haven't got around to fixing it;
at night the coyotes howl down at the reservoir.

Linda's gone off to Idaho – again.
God, I miss her! Even
the rows and her goddamn nagging.

My mattress lies inside the door.
We're on Hollywood's doorstep –
I like it here.

Peru

Temple of the Sun
between us and the Pacific –
vultures

driving south –
machine shops replaced
by artichoke fields

dunes all along this coast   no keys in my pocket

higher altitude   a chorus of dogs sings us to sleep

paddling in the Pacific   pelicans surf the waves

did your ancestors please the Incas here too, ibis?

flamingos on a salt lake
above the Andes and the sky –
inverted monocular

Chinchero –
a yellow butterfly heads north
towards the noonday sun

waxing moon   first glimpse of the glacier

meeting of the rivers   how long before it melts?

in the shade of the glacier
this pale green grass –
is it frost-covered?

the mist finally lifts
revealing its grandeur –
Machu Picchu

A Morning in Yacango

It's Day Five of our Peruvian road trip during which we visit several sites of Inca and other ancient civilisations. We make an excursion from the town of Moquegua towards the mountain of Cerro Baúl, which has the ruins of a Wari administrative centre on its summit. The mountain bears a striking resemblance to Ben Bulben, which towers over the town of Sligo back home in Ireland.

> after climbing
> my grandfather
> dies suddenly

My three travelling companions set off to climb Cerro Baúl. Because of a recent knee operation, I can't join them, so they drop me off in the nearby village of Yacango. Today is the feast day of the village's patron, *Señor de Gran Poder* (Lord of Great Power), and there is a Mass at 11 O'Clock. I stroll down to the church and catch the second half.

I feel conspicuous as the only *gringa,* and a little disrespectful in my shorts. Some of the parishioners smile at me, others give me suspicious looks. I follow them up to where a figure of the crucified Christ rests on a bed of baby blue gauze on a portable wooden platform near the altar. He is wearing a richly embroidered blood-red velvet scarf. We touch it in turn.

> old habits
> sign of the cross
> die hard

Ecuador

Puerto Lopez:
pelicans take turns
diving in the shallows

on the beachfront
a barefoot man bounces
his pink-swaddled babe

he takes the whale's tail
threads a leather thong through it –
my new necklace

Guayaquíl Cathedral –
she kisses her rabbit
before the dying Christ

the furry burr
that was in my sneaker
unfurls, shimmies away

three hours on the bus   suddenly an ostrich

transporting us into cloud, into forest   a cable car

cathedral café
beside the cakes & nougat –
communion wafers

homesickness –
I open the balcony door
let this strange city in

Santay Island crocodile:
his jaw's shadow about to eat
my shadow

Galápagos Islands

morning excursion –
the head of a sea turtle
pops up out of blue

alighting on an outcrop
a yellow warbler
lives up to his name

hot afternoon
he blends in well with the basalt –
lava lizard

the pelican swoops down
lands on our lifeboat –
hunter's moon

wetlands   ripples spreading out from the flamingo

sea lion underwater his backflip too fast for photos

the tropical fish
that lived in my uncle's house –
I'm in their tank now

Dateline Quito

It is a bright October morning in the Ecuadorian capital. In the guesthouse, I am having breakfast at the same time as a very large American gentleman who is around my age. After some silence, I try to make polite conversation over fried eggs and watered-down juice.

I mention how much I enjoyed visiting the Church of the Compañia yesterday, with its lavish gold-foiled interiors. He recommends a different church which has less gold but is (apparently) more important historically. Right so.

The conversation turns to Peru. He takes great pleasure in telling me that the trip he and his wife made to Machu Picchu five years ago only cost half what mine did last month. Right so. He brandishes the word 'wife' like a Jedi sword. She's not with him on this occasion.

>   just after the visit
>   to the giant metal Virgin –
>   storm breaking

Scenes from Peru & Ecuador
(for Uzma and i.m. of her friend Ghazala)

With his song, the crooner tries to connect
over lunch, where the Nazca lines connect.

The Cuzceñan haiku poet, sharing
his favourite Japanese master, connects.

At Machu Picchu, after the mist clears,
a young Israeli takes our photo to connect.

Pedro and I banter while our flight is delayed:
he wonders if the Incas had help, connected.

The toddler who held back from chatting, smiling,
fist bumps me when we say goodbye; we connect.

Californian Mike tells me about the twenty veterans
who take their own lives each day, who disconnect.

At Puerto Lopez, the artist-in-residence shows
us his garden, his cabins, his paintings – connected.

After the whale-watching trip, the seasick woman
tells me she's a missionary, connecting.

I ask Bonnie if she believes in evolution:
I'm a Christian, those fossils aren't connected.

The old German lady at the Quito traffic lights
warns me in English about pick-pockets who connect.

She whose names mean *one who intoxicates,*
one-eyed woman of sorrows, yearns to re-connect.

Colombia

an old man rummages
in Bogotá bins –
travel-weary

road closure:
on his cracked phone screen
a fatal landslide

rushing to lunch
I pass a homeless woman –
her sparkly sandals

poised for flight
around my niece's home –
Hallowe'en bats

All Saints' Day:
a small superman costume
on the *barrio* balcony

father's anniversary   first glimpse of the Caribbean

night of Cohen's death   salsa dancing my grief

Botero's bronze nudes:
their eyes identical
to their nipples

valley hike   wax palm trees all across the horizon

at the tour's end   Pablo Escobar's gravelled grave

last meal here –
my lettuce leaf a butterfly
about to take flight

The Rules of Salsa

1. Warm up beforehand.
2. Let the man lead.
3. Stay relaxed.
4. Let the man lead.
5. Take small steps.
6. Let the man lead.
7. Maintain your balance.
8. Let the man lead.
9. Tie your hair up.
10. Let the man lead.
11. Keep a straight torso.
12. Let the man lead.
13. Swing those hips!
14. Let the man lead.
15. Shoulders down.
16. Let the man lead.
17. Turn on a dime.
18. Let the man lead.
19. Never refuse a dance.
20. LET THE MAN LEAD!

Santiago, Chile

Plaza de Armas
under the jacaranda –
a selfied couple

sound check   his *duduk* notes infusing the studio

Neruda's house   his pen, glasses, medals under glass

I turn the page
pressing this purple bloom –
Italian novel

III East

Resettled

> arrival in Sydney –
> Christmas tree baubles glint
> in the summer sun

Twelve years and the Irish Sea separated me from my cousin Catherine growing up. We didn't see much of each other, although our mothers always remained close. She and her husband moved from the UK to a Melbourne suburb two years ago to be nearer to their two children and four grandchildren. They invite me to come and stay when they hear I'll be in Australia.

On Day One, which is a Sunday, I meet them *en masse*. Smothered in sunscreen, we enjoy lunch in the garden. Catherine's family members are warm, welcoming, and good fun, like herself and her mother Billie before her.

> in the neighbour's tree
> overlooking our reunion –
> a fake koala

Day Two is another scorcher. Catherine and I go for a walk along the beach promenade and are enveloped by the heat and the many flies.

The temperature drops by twenty degrees Celsius on Day Three, a not uncommon occurrence in Melbourne. I spend the day exploring the city, hopping on and off a tour bus.

On Day Four, my last full day here, Catherine and I drive down the scenic Mornington Peninsula. We stop off at Arthur's Seat where we have a great view of Port Philip Bay.

> growing wild here
> both our mothers' favourite –
> freesias

Over lunch, we reminisce about the O'Connors, and how much animated chat and laughter was heard whenever a critical mass of the ten sisters (and one brother) got together. Although he was one of ten himself, my Dad used to wonder how they ever managed to hear each other: *they all keep talking at the same time!* There are only three of them left now.

> my grandfather's signature
> on the 1911 Census –
> so like mother's

Japan

Shinobazu Pond –
even these withered lotuses
can lift my heart

heated toilet seat –
memories of growing up
in a large family

deep-fried pork:
I await instructions
on how to eat it

we look through the dark
to the place where Mount Fuji
is supposed to be

arrival in Kyoto...
I buy flowers for myself
flowers for the Buddha

the clunk of wooden sandals
on stone paving –
Mount Otowa

thatched with water reeds
topped with acer leaves –
Basho-an, the poet's hut

further uphill
autumn birdsong leads the way -
Buson's grave

wandering poet's well   its stone collar a lotus

dusk over the city   two small girls in flowery *kimono*

A Slice of Autumn

The journey from Kyoto to Nara is just under an hour by train. The burnt colours of the trees that we speed past are stunning, and I find myself thinking about *Autumn Leaves,* a French song from the forties with lyrics by the poet Jacques Prévert. But it is just the air, by Joseph Kosma, that I can't help myself from humming.

The man sitting opposite me asks me if I'm French, having recognised the song, and we get chatting. Turns out he's a Vietnamese-born French citizen, an elderly gent called Paul who loves to travel in Japan. By the time we reach Nara, we have decided to do some sight-seeing together.

Uphill from the train station, we see two men taking turns pounding rice into paste with wooden mallets outside a shop. The green paste is then moulded into biscuit shapes and baked in an oven. The result is *mochi,* a typical rice cake.

   tea ceremony —
   the *kimono*-clad woman
   folds, refolds the napkin

Our journey takes us through Nara Park, where hundreds of tame deer roam. Regarded as messengers of the gods in the Shinto tradition, they have protected status which allows them to wander freely. They bow their heads to visitors who feed them with special crackers sold at shops and stalls nearby.

   soft gingko nuts
   same colour as their foliage —
   sushi bar

We spend the next couple of hours visiting temples and shrines, and taking photographs in the clear light of this crisp, sunny day. One of the largest seated Buddhas in the world is to be found at Todaji Temple, one of the world's oldest wooden structures. It's a popular spot, with tourists buying mala beads, miniature prayer wheels and other Buddhist paraphernalia at the busy shop inside.

> bronze Buddha. . .
> cameras pointed away from
> the ugly wooden statue

Kofukuji Temple is also striking, with its five- and seven-storey pagodas. I see something there which I've never seen before in any place of worship: a woman ladling water onto a standing statue. I later discover that the figure is that of Kannon, Japan's version of the Buddhist deity of compassion, which takes a female form here.

Close to the entrance to our last shrine of the day, four women are diligently clearing the pathway. They wear matching pale pink tops, black aprons and an assortment of hats. Two of them sweep dead leaves into orange plastic dustpans with their old-fashioned brooms. The third pours the pan's contents into a box with rope handles, and the fourth hoists it onto her shoulder and walks away.

> Shinto shrine:
> a fierce dragon guards
> the purifying font

Hong Kong

Star Ferry entrance   a grey-haired couple shares a joke

giant Buddha gesturing towards the waxing moon

sampan journey –
no bird ever sings
in these cages

trying to compete
with skyscrapers' Xmas lights –
half moon

viewing tower
in the rooftop pool below –
a lone swimmer

a hundred and ten years
after the big typhoon –
typhoon shelter

impossible to get
the sunset shot –
South China Sea

Kathmandu

halfway through my trip –
afternoon sun reflected
on the gold *stupa*

giant prayer wheel:
slowing down for the old guy
speeding up for the youngsters

Pashupatinath Temple   the squeaking of monkeys

they burn night and day   riverside funeral pyres

Buddhas of Asia

After seeing the world's largest indoor seated bronze Buddha at Nara,
I visit the largest outdoor seated bronze Buddha outside Hong Kong.
This difference is important: big Buddhas mean big business –
everyone wants a piece of His calm. Later I see the smallest
Buddha in the world, through a magnifying glass placed
behind more glass, in a temple in Colombo;
not long after I stumble upon the casket
bearing some of His skullbone relics
in the National Museum of India
where I learn that He had had
an early aniconic phase: His
only representations then
the Wheel of Dharma,
an empty throne,
the Bodhi tree,

footprints…

New Delhi

new year   the peacock struts through a junkyard

in trees above the empty swimming pool   crows

narrow laneway
pictures of various gods
at pissing level

from the *tuk tuk*
between buildings and trees –
a flash of full moon

New Year at Rumtek Monastery

We hike an hour to reach this special place
to see first-hand the sacred lama dance.
For ten full hours they never slacken pace
as one by one we're drawn into their trance.

Sustained by snacks, free cups of butter tea,
we marvel at the costumes and the hats,
the players of the horns, the drums, *uzme,*
their masks adorned with multi-coloured plaits.

A special day, Aquarius new moon,
of this pure spectacle we never tire;
with *Losar,* the Tibetan New Year, soon,
they toss the wrathful god into the fire.

Because of this auspicious conflagration,
we're free next year from every obscuration.

Sikkim Retreat

lighting the road to our retreat   waxing wolf moon

less cloudy today   first sight of Kanchenjunga

thunderclap!
the new prayer flags
get their first blessing

walking meditation...
the cream-coloured butterfly
circles me twice

lunchtime salad:
the spring onion becomes
a hot green chilli!

steep ascent to the gate
sound of the wind –
my beating heart

afternoon tea break...
strains of Bollywood music
floating uphill

early morning song
of a Himalayan bird:
I'm over here. Here!

teaching on emptiness
the curtain fills
for a short while

evening meditation   howling jackals break our silence

3am thunderstorm   its silent aftermath

morning silence –
inside, pans clattering
outside, the thrush's song

breakfast outdoors:
would you like some scrambled egg
little green spider?

last day of retreat –
gusts of wind release leaves
onto the newly-swept path

Morning Practice
(for Dónal C.)

The leaves: I'm sweeping them but still they fall
upon the steps and all along the path –
I wonder if I'll reach the boundary wall.

The storm last night increased my brush's haul,
though for this rain they will say *dhanyavaad,*
I'm sweeping up the leaves and still they fall.

How fine to hear the dark blue song thrush call
while smaller birds enjoy their dusty bath –
they're sure to reach and pass the boundary wall.

Sometimes I think I'll never clear them all –
like Milarepa fearing Marpa's wrath –
so still I'm sweeping leaves and still they fall.

From here in Sikkim via West Bengal,
my pilgrimage goes on into Sarnath,
I plan to make it inside Deer Park's wall.

I hope this spell in detail I'll recall,
once I progress into its aftermath.
Meanwhile I'm sweeping leaves but still they fall,
I don't know if I'll reach the boundary wall.

Agra

en route from Delhi
the monsoon has yielded
yellow mustard flowers

double-domed mausoleum   the hum of awed visitors

sunrise over the lesser wife's red-brick tomb

all the way from Jaipur
carried on camel carts –
these inlaid marbles

Taj Mahal in the distance a parrot lands on a palm

Mughal fort   children in red rolling down its grass hills

European traveller:
his cigarette smoke rising
above the cannon

Baby Taj Mahal
gift of an abandoned daughter –
pomegranate flower

Varanasi

a shirtless man and I
bow to each other –
ashram entrance

a cigarette booth
by the mango wood stockpile
for the pyres

Manikarnika Ghat   cremations lit by Shiva's fire

dusk over the Ganges   kites spinning

even inside
this guesthouse bedroom –
the great Ganesh

evening *puja:*
the bells' peals echo
across the sacred river

narrow laneway
smells of incense and cowshit –
leaving Benares

Mumbai

muggy morning   these fan blades slice the Bombay air

Gateway to India   yet another request for a selfie

sunset over the harbour
no Bombay Gin
at this hotel bar

last day in India –
seagulls accompany our boat
back to shore

Endangered

The group dynamic on this bus tour is rather strange, with friendships forming, dissolving and reforming daily.

> mid-point –
> he tells me I've got
> the wrong end of the stick

Towards the end of the week, we visit one of Sri Lanka's larger national parks. The guide assigned to our jeep is very enthusiastic and calls all the deer 'Bambi'. There's a lot of stopping and starting, a lot of false alarms. At one stage he points out a shuddering bush which may or may not have been shaken by a bear.

> first safari –
> a crocodile-shaped cloud
> reflected in the lily pond

No animal corpses were found here in Yala National Park after the 2004 tsunami as they all made their way up to higher ground in time. However, our guide quietly mentions that around 250 people died here in that disaster, including a man who was his colleague and friend. The smile he's been wearing all afternoon disappears.

> first and last swim
> in the Indian Ocean –
> a bigger wave knocks us

Sri Lanka

after traveller's tummy –
a calming breakfast
by the Laccadive Sea

handbag-free
no iPhone to count my steps –
beach walk

Gangaramaya shrine...
an old lady adds some jasmine
to our flower tray

accompanying us
uphill to the sacred footprint –
frog tones

the temple's lily pond
stripped of its blooms –
full moon day

chatter in the tour bus stops   tsunami damage

storm breaking we circumambulate the wishing *stupa*

Barcelona

morning shower
the balloon-sellers and I
shelter in the bandstand

laughter...
under his bushy beard
a dimple

fabulous sunset over Sitges   tipsy on gin

Güell Palace   mosaic turrets reach into cloud

Magnus's Digit

You've cast your finger aside
where the freesias are fading,
the wisteria is wilting,
and the roses are in full bloom.

It sits on the garden's stone table,
next to the candle in the jam jar,
but is this unfired phallus
of clay a thumb or a middle?

Either way, it's your gift to us,
left behind in this old farmhouse.
Our projects trundle on, while yours
hitches us on to each new breakfast.

It wasn't too ambitious but, in truth,
there's been a fair bit of partying,
with your crowd supplying the soap
bubbles, the glitter and the guitar strings.

We miss the trundle of your skateboards
on the tiles, and the handmade dream-
catchers, not so much the piano
practice or the overflowing ashtrays.

But, as well as being back in Oslo,
you're still here, in a way,
your legacy a daily message
of *Well done!* or even *Up yours!*

Can Serrat / Montserrat

first cross –
she scoops up red dust
for her artist's suitcase

path of flowering thyme
around the corner
a disused tile factory

silver tunnel
under these trees
dandelion clusters

two chatterboxes
silenced by poppies
in the olive grove

Ave Maria Lane:
its dark narrow route
lit by pilgrims' candles

paper lantern
casting a moving shadow
on these last pages

Thinking about our Bodies at the Rodin Museum

It's hard not to think about bodies here –
all those torsos and thighs of marble and bronze!
I long for us to merge like the earth
and the moon, to taste the kiss of Paolo
and Francesca in a cloudy entwinement:
my hand resting on the curve of your buttock,
your face covering my breast.

I want to get lost
in you rather than in thought
or despair. I yearn to become
your consort, your concubine,
your soft, insatiable woman,

your flame. Later I pass the lovers' locks
for sale on the quay – how many couples
have chained their troth here on Pont Neuf? –
and recall again the chaste embrace
of our forms sculpted in flesh and bone.

A Lapsed Catholic's Prayer

or two, or three,
or try twenty, said
in twenty churches
and cathedrals, all
along St. James's
way, with rows
of matching flame-wax.

On a May day
I come to rest
in Notre Dame
as choral notes
drift upwards
to kiss a trio
of glass roses.

(i.m. Sr. Maureen O'Sullivan 1920-2017)

Envoi: Back Home

Settling

after this world trip
my aunt cautions me
crossing her road

thanks for seeing me safely home   June moon

back on the refilled bird-feeder   greenfinch

awake in my bed
the strange, familiar noise
of trains passing

dusting deckchairs   the start of an Irish summer

another suitcase   the sneakers left behind too tight

the watch that's travelled
and the one that hasn't
both tell the same time

rehung mirror
catching evening light –
midsummer

Wild Atlantic Way

after a Corrib dip
ducklings snuggle into mother...
each other

Eyre Square   a seagull eyes up my tuna sandwich

Jungle Café   a robin pecks at my cake crumbs

Just past Mayo's fjord   newly-shorn sheep

we hear them   then see them   Westport swifts

forecast wrong again   swans on the Garavogue

free jazz gig   I make this fizzy shandy last

moisture-laden clouds
over Roscommon fields –
dry stone walls

the rain that's held off
comes hurtling down –
Queen Maeve's grave

Glossary

Santiago de Compostela (page 46): The *botafumeiro* is a famous thurible in the Santiago de Compostela Cathedral. Incense is burned in this large swinging metal container.

Santiago, Chile (page 66): The *duduk* is an ancient double-reed woodwind flute made of apricot wood. It is indigenous to Armenia.

Kathmandu (page 77) and **Sri Lanka (page 93):** a *stupa* is a round structure containing relics of Buddhist clergy, that is used as a place of meditation.

New Delhi (page 79): a *tuk tuk* is an auto rickshaw in India.

New Year at Rumtek Monastery (page 80): The *uzme* is the lead chanter at Tibetan Buddhist prayer ceremonies.

Morning Practice (page 85): 1. *dhanyavaad* is one of the Hindi words for 'thank you'. 2. **Marpa** and **Milarepa** were two lineage holders of the Kagyu school of Tibetan Buddhism who lived in the late 10th century. Marpa was Milarepa's guru and was famously hard on him. Milarepa was also a yogi and communicated in poetry and song.

Agra (page 87): The **Mughal Empire** was an empire in the Indian subcontinent, founded in 1526. It was established and ruled by a Muslim dynasty.

Varanasi (page 89): A *puja* is a prayer ritual performed by Hindus and Buddhists to host, honour and worship one or more deities, or to spiritually celebrate an event.

Acknowledgements & Thanks

Journals:
Thanks are due to the editors of the following journals in which many pieces of work in this collection, or earlier versions of them, were first published: *Abridged, A Hundred Gourds, All The Sins, Blithe Spirit* (the journal of the British Haiku Society), *cattails* (the journal of the United Haiku and Tanka Society), *Chrysanthemum, Dodging the Rain, Failed Haiku – A Journal of English Senryu, hedgerow: a journal of short poems, The Honest Ulsterman, Icebox* (Hailstone Haiku Circle, Kyoto), *Kō* (Japan), *Kokako* (New Zealand), *Many Roads* (the Bodhicharya e-magazine), *Moongarlic, Other Terrain Journal* (Swinburne University, Australia), *Poetry 24, Presence, Revival* (the journal of the Limerick Writers' Centre), *Skylight 47, Sonic Boom, Spilling Cocoa over Martin Amis, Stepaway Magazine, The Taj Mahal Review* (India), *Textualia* (Peru), *The Heron's Nest* and *The Irish Times*.

Anthologies:
her bony back was included in *evolution:The Red Moon Anthology of English-Language Haiku* 2010 (Red Moon Press, 2011). It also appeared in *Initial Response* (2011). It is included in the forthcoming two anthologies: *Wild Voices 2* (Wildflower Poetry Press, 2017) and a women's haiku anthology forthcoming from Jacar Press. *rainy afternoon, first-ever taste* and *boat tour of the port* appear in *Stone after Stone*, the Haiku Ireland members' anthology (The Fishing Cat Press, 2017). *at the pier's end* was published in *Red Lamp, Black Piano,* the anthology of the Cáca Milis Cabaret (Tara Press, 2013). *fifty-something* will appear in *Wild Voices*

2 (Wildflower Poetry Press, 2017) and in *Beyond Words,* an English-Bulgarian anthology, jointly published by the British Haiku Society and the Bulgarian Haiku Union (2017). *memorial gardens* will be included in a women's haiku anthology fothcoming from Jacar Press. *grey day* was published in *Beginning,* the British Haiku Society's members' anthology 2016. *waxing June moon* will appear in *Beyond Words,* an English-Bulgarian anthology, jointly published by the British Haiku Society and the Bulgarian Haiku Union (2017). *lane swimming* appears in *dust devils, The Red Moon Anthology of English-Language Haiku* 2016 (Red Moon Press, 2017). *Botero's bronze nudes* appears in *Ekphrasis,* the British Haiku Society's Members' Anthology 2017.

Awards:
her bony back won the Haiku Ireland Kukai 2: 2010 and was published in *Stone after Stone,* the Haiku Ireland members' anthology (The Fishing Cat Press, 2017). *after the reading* won the Haiku Ireland Kukai 3: 2015 and was published in *Stone after Stone,* the Haiku Ireland members' anthology (The Fishing Cat Press, 2017). *Sandymount Strand* was shortlisted for the Museum of Haiku Literature Award in the May 2017 issue of *Blithe Spirit,* the journal of the British Haiku Society, having first appeared in its February 2017 issue. *Leaving Vigo* was nominated by *Revival Literary Journal* for a Forward Prize for Best Single Poem in 2014. *All Saints' Day* was shortlisted for the H. Gene Murtha Memorial Senryu Contest 2017, judged jointly by the editors of the *Failed Haiku* and *Prune Juice* senryu journals.

Residencies:
I spent the month of April 2017 working on my manuscript at the Can Serrat Artists' Centre outside Barcelona, and would like to thank them for the partial scholarship towards that residency, and for the sunny welcome. I'd also like to express gratitude to the Arts Council of Ireland / An Chomhairle Ealaíon for awarding me a travel & training grant towards that residency.

I spent a week at the Tyrone Guthrie Centre at Annaghmakerrig in County Monaghan in June 2016, and wish to express my appreciation to them for also providing a comfortable space in which to work.

Other thanks:
My thanks are due to members of the following groups for their inputs into work I shared with them at our various meetings: the Hibernian Poetry Workshop, Haiku Ireland and Jim Norton's haibun group. Neil Brosnan and Seán O'Connor offered astute critiques of individual pieces. I'd like to offer special thanks to those individuals who gave valuable feedback on the entire manuscript: Amanda Bell, Maurice Devitt, Nessa O'Mahony and John Saunders, and to the authors of the back page comments: David Burleigh, Caroline Skanne and Breda Wall Ryan.

Appreciation is also due to my fellow Poetry Divas: Kate Dempsey, Barbara Smith and Triona Walsh, for the cheerleading, fun and wisdom. Many thanks to everyone who extended the hands of hospitality and friendship to me in 2016 and 2017 – far too numerous to mention but you know who you are! Likewise my travel champions.

About the Author

Dubliner Maeve O'Sullivan works as a tutor of journalism and creative writing in further education. Her haiku and poems have been widely published, anthologised and awarded, and have been translated into ten languages. *Double Rainbow* (with Kim Richardson) was published by Alba Publishing in 2005, as was Maeve's first solo collection of haiku poetry, *Initial Response,* in 2011.

Her collection of long-form poetry, *Vocal Chords,* was published in 2014, and her second solo collection of haiku, *A Train Hurtles West,* was published in 2015, both by Alba Publishing. Maeve is a founder of Haiku Ireland, and a long-standing member of the British Haiku Society. She is also a member of the Hibernian Poetry Workshop and the Poetry Divas spoken word collective, which performs at festivals and other events. You can find her on Twitter @writefromwithin. Travel tweets and photos can be found using the hashtag #gacháiteile.